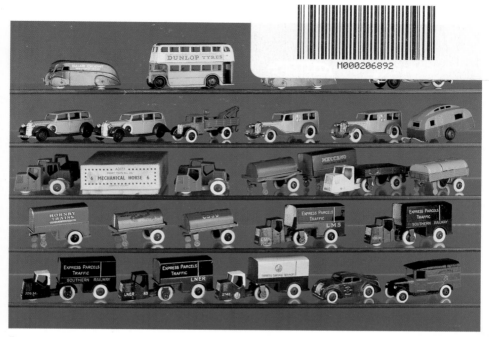

Rare pre-war commercial vehicles. Unusual models from the 1930s, including the short-lived Holland Coachcraft Van (top left) and the Airmail Car (blue) (bottom right).

DINKY TOYS

David Cooke

The Shire Book

Published in 2005 by Shire Publications Ltd,
Cromwell House, Church Street, Princes Risborough,
Buckinghamshire HP27 9AA, UK.
(Website: www.shirebooks.co.uk)

British Library Cataloguing in Publication Data:
Cooke, David
Dinky Toys
1. Dinky Toys
2. Dinky Toys – Collectors and collecting
I. Title 688.7′2
ISBN 0 7478 0427 3

Cover: *A selection of Dinky Toys with shop display material.*

For Cecil Gibson and Mike and Sue Richardson, who reawakened and consolidated my
interest in Dinky Toys.

ACKNOWLEDGEMENTS
The author would like to thank all the collectors and enthusiasts who have provided him
with information and checked details, especially John Ramsay and Derek Barratt; the very
helpful staff at Shire Publications; David Ross, who photographed most of the models; Nigel
Mynheer of Christie's for the loan of photographs; but most of all his own family, who have
encouraged and helped him produce this book.
The photographs on pages 1, 11 (top), 12 (bottom), 13 (bottom), 14, 15 (both), 24 (bottom), 34, 37
(top) and 39 (bottom) are reproduced by kind permission of Christie's, and that on page 19 by
kind permission of Eastern Counties Newspapers Ltd.

Printed in Great Britain by CIT Printing Services Ltd,
Press Buildings, Merlins Bridge, Haverfordwest,
Pembrokeshire SA61 1XF.

CONTENTS

Four of the 900 series of Dinky Supertoys: (left to right) Leyland Octopus Flat Truck with Chains; Leyland Eight-wheeled Chassis on test; Foden 14-Ton Tanker 'Regent'; Leyland Shell-BP Fuel Tanker.

CHRONOLOGY OF THE HISTORY OF MECCANO LTD AND DINKY TOYS

1863   Frank Hornby born (15th May).
1901   Hornby patents and produces 'Mechanics Made Easy' (later called Meccano).
1907   Meccano name registered (14th September).
1912   Meccano France founded.
1914   Binns Road factory, Liverpool, opened.
1916   *Meccano Magazine* first issued.
1920   Hornby O gauge trains introduced.
1923   Railway Accessories introduced.
1931   Modelled Miniatures (MM) introduced.
1934   MM renamed Dinky Toys.
1936   Frank Hornby died aged seventy-three (21st September).
1938   Hornby-Dublo Trains introduced.
1941   Meccano production ceased owing to Second World War.
1946   Production of Dinky Toys recommenced.
1947   Dinky Supertoys introduced.
1956   Corgi Toys introduced ('the ones with windows').
1958   The first Dinky Toy with windows introduced.
1964   Dinky Toys (GB) purchased by Lines Bros (Tri-ang).
1971   Lines Bros in liquidation. Meccano Ltd bought by Airfix.
1979   Binns Road factory closed and UK production ceased (30th November).
1980   Some models continued to be manufactured abroad (e.g. Hong Kong).
1985   Kenner Parker Toys Inc became the new owner of Dinky Toys.
1987   Dinky Toys trade name sold to Universal International, Hong Kong.
1988   The 'Dinky Collection' introduced.
1992   Tyco Toys Inc acquired Universal Matchbox including the Dinky Toys brand name.
1996   Mattel Inc merged with Tyco Toys.

514 Guy Weetabix Van. This model was introduced in June 1952 and probably deleted in 1954, a relatively short production run. This particular toy was the prototype with hand-painted lettering only on the front and nearside of the body. The offside was left unmarked.

DINKY TOYS – 'A FASCINATING HOBBY'

In December 1934 the *Meccano Magazine* published an article entitled 'Collecting Meccano Dinky Toys: A New and Fascinating Hobby'. The name 'Dinky Toys' had first appeared in 1934, superseding 'Modelled Miniatures' as the title of the range of metal toys, introduced in 1931, made by Meccano, the company that also manufactured Meccano outfits, Hornby Trains and Railway Accessories. Several manufacturers, mostly outside Britain, were already producing models similar in concept to Dinky Toys, the idea having been pioneered by Tootsietoys in the United States in the 1930s and later adopted by Solido in France and Märklin in Germany.

All these diecast products were about the same size and scale and proved instantly popular with children throughout the world. There were many reasons for their success. There was an extensive range of models (especially Dinky Toys); they were often miniature versions of actual vehicles, and all types of vehicles, road, rail, sea and air, were modelled. They were usually small enough to be held in the hand or pocket; most had freely rotating road wheels so that they could be pushed around easily, and they were often brightly coloured and had an intrinsic charm. Whole series and fleets could be collected, and new models were eagerly awaited by collectors. They were strong, well made, lasted almost indefinitely and had considerable play value. Displays and dioramas were suggested in magazines, leaflets and catalogues. They were cheap to buy and were often purchased as birthday or Christmas presents. Dinky Toys in particular would be exported throughout the world.

In recent decades the small boys who owned these models, now

Nine small vans from the 1950s. (Front, from left) 465 Morris Commercial; 470/1/2 Austin. (Back, from left) 480/1/2 Bedford; 490/1 Electric Dairy Van.

The 400 series of medium-size trucks: Bedford S-type (two) (left); Bedford Articulated; Leyland Comet (three versions) and Commer Breakdown Truck.

grown into affluent middle age, have been filled with nostalgia for the childhood toys that gave them so many hours of fun. Intent on reviving memories of manoeuvring buses around the living-room carpet, a fleet of lorries in the sandpit or racing cars in the school playground, they have clamoured to purchase surviving examples. While these solid playthings survived most of those hazardous activities, many rarer models are today valued at hundreds of pounds and never venture beyond the glass display cabinet.

Dinky Toys appeared to have a monopoly in their field, possessing all the qualities just described, and because of the huge range of different items in their catalogue, up to three hundred at any one time, collectors throughout the British Empire were keen to extend their miniature fleets. The diecast toys were tough. Although a few pre-war toys were made of lead, the majority were manufactured in an alloy called Mazak (or Zamak in the United States), which was almost unbreakable. The alloy consisted of 96 per cent zinc, with smaller quantities of aluminium, copper and magnesium. The process was imported from the United States and copied the methods of an American toy company, Dowst, which had made Tootsietoys in the early 1930s. Led by Dinky Toys, British manufacturers excelled in this industry, both before the Second World War and into the 1950s and beyond, when they were joined by Corgi, Matchbox and Britain's Toys. Unfortunately, many of the pre-war Mazak toys now suffer from so-called metal fatigue, intercrystalline corrosion, due to poor ingredient control. Experiments by Dinky Toys to improve castings and reduce costs resulted in a few models being made in aluminium or plastic.

At Meccano's Binns Road factory in Liverpool huge pieces of expensive machinery were installed to ensure a perfect product. Diecasting is the process of forcing molten metal into an extremely accurate die or mould, and when the metal has cooled and solidified the resulting castings are trimmed, cleaned and enamelled.

The toys were painted in bright, often unrealistic colours and can be identified by the names 'Dinky Toys' or 'Meccano Ltd' on the chassis, and sometimes by the model name and number as well or instead. For

Pre-war boxes from the 42 to 47 series. (From left) 44 AA Set, with 43a RAC Call Box; 47d Belisha Beacons; 45 Garage (with Chrysler Airflow); 42a Police Hut (with post-war trade box). Note the RAC Set is similar to the AA Set. Set 46 is a Pavement Set.

further identification and protection the model was packed in its own box or in some cases with others as part of a gift set. There is an enormous variety of Dinky Toy boxes in cardboard and, later, plastic. Pre-war boxes are now very rare and much sought after by collectors.

The finished products were then dispatched to the retailer, who was supplied with Dinky Toys marketing material. Dealers received merchandising items such as glass cabinets, catalogues, price lists and special metal price tags, and their shelves were fully stocked with boxes of Dinky Toys. Until about 1954 so-called 'trade boxes', usually containing six individual models, often in different colours, provided the buyer with a huge choice. Thereafter, Dinky Toys came in individual boxes.

Trade boxes. 25 series commercial vehicles. 25b Covered Wagon (Carter Paterson) (back); 25d Petrol Tank Wagon (Mobiloil) (front); 25e Tipping Wagon (right); 25f Market Gardener's Wagon (left); with pre-war trade boxes (containing six toys) for 25d and 25f.

1:40 scale 23 series racing cars. Post-war continuation of a pre-war series. (Front row, left to right) 23k (230) Talbot-Lago; 23n (231) Maserati; 23f (232) Alfa Romeo; 23g (233) Cooper-Bristol; 23h (234) Ferrari. (Back row, left to right) 23j (235) HWM; 236 Connaught; 237 Mercedes-Benz; 238 Jaguar; 239 Vanwall.

The majority of Dinky Toys were around 10 cm (4 inches) long, and the bigger Dinky Supertoys, mostly larger trucks and lorries (called 'wagons' in the 1940s and 1950s), were up to 20 cm (8 inches) long. The scales of the toys varied considerably, from the smallest ships, about 4 cm ($1^1/2$ inches) long, to a very large lawnmower, one-eighth of its actual size. The more common scales used are listed here, with some examples of models made to each scale:

1:1800	ships
1:200	aeroplanes (early)
1:75	aeroplanes, average (1965–80)
1:72	(OO gauge) some buses, figures and pre-war small cars; 'Dublo' models from 1957 onwards
1:60	military vehicles (1953–71)
1:48	the majority of Dinky Toys between 1949 and 1961
1:43	(O gauge) a standard scale
1:40	farm vehicles and racing cars (230–5)
1:35	cars (1977–80)
1:32	racing cars (1970–80); military vehicles (1968–80)
1:25	Ford Capri
1:8	lawnmower

The model usually consisted of one or two parts: the fewer the parts, the cheaper it was to produce. A basic model car of the 1950s comprised a one-piece body with a tinplate chassis, to which were attached two metal axles, diecast wheels and rubber tyres. The chassis gave the manufacturer's name and brief details of the model. The body and chassis were riveted together. There are exceptions to this system, particularly in

Continuous development. 40 and 140 series British cars and their successors. (Back row from left) 40e (153) Standard; 40g (159) Morris; 40d (152) Austin; 140b (156) Rover 75 (two); 40j (161) Austin Somerset; 162 Ford Zephyr. (Front row from left) Vauxhall Victor; Humber Hawk; Ford Anglia; Ford Escort (two).

models from the 1930s, but it applies to the majority of Dinky Toys.

More expensive toys, such as the larger trucks, consisted of two body parts, the cab and chassis from one mould and the container component from the other, together with a smaller tinplate baseplate beneath the cab. Occasionally, the two body pieces were joined together by a small nut and screw instead of by permanent rivets.

In the final decade of Dinky Toy production, techniques improved so much that the manufacturing process included a complete diecast or plastic chassis, many other plastic parts such as windows, seating, wheels and grilles, and an enormous variety of operating items like doors, bonnets, tipping mechanisms, cranes, elevators and even flashing direction indicators. These sophisticated toys had advanced a long way from their basic humble beginnings in the 1930s. Prices, however, remained within the reach of children, for whom they were intended. During the first decade of production the price of individual Dinky Toys was in the range of sixpence to one shilling, although one set containing eight large aeroplanes cost seven shillings. During the 1950s the average price was about three shillings for small cars, lorries and buses, while the larger Supertoys cost around seven shillings and sixpence to nine shillings.

Towards the end of production in the late 1970s the newly decimalised prices ranged from £1.50 for cars, vans and small trucks to £5 for large items such as spaceships, fire engines and military vehicles.

Early sets. These Dinky Toy sets developed from the Modelled Miniatures series introduced in 1931. 1 Station Staff (back left); 3 Passengers (back centre, in incorrect box); 4 Engineering Staff (back right); 5 Train and Hotel Staff (centre); 6 Shepherd Set (front centre). Also shown: 12d Telegraph Messenger (right) and 760 Pillar Box (left).

THE PRE-WAR YEARS (1931–41)

Hornby Railway Accessories had been available as additions to the O gauge Hornby Trains since 1923 and had proved very popular with model-railway enthusiasts. The range was expanded with items such as platform machines, station name boards, water tanks and a watchman's hut. The *Meccano Magazine* stated in December 1931 that these accessories 'effect a surprisingly great improvement in appearance!' (to layouts).

However, there was also a demand for miniature railwaymen and passengers, so in that same month Hornby introduced the first toys that were to develop into the great Dinky Toys brand. This set, named Modelled Miniatures No. 1, consisting of six station staff, was the precursor of millions of toys that would continue to be available for the next fifty years.

By the time of the publication of the September 1932 edition of the *Meccano Magazine* this first set had been joined by further sets consisting mainly of passengers and staff. Set No. 21, a locomotive with four wagons, was unusual in that it was the first Hornby toy to be manufactured in a much smaller scale, running on wheels and made in solid metal rather than the larger tinplate O gauge trains. It was not until December 1933 that one of the most significant sets was introduced: Set No. 22 was made up of six road vehicles – two cars, a van, a pick-up, a tractor and a tank. They were sold in a boxed set costing four shillings. Later, each model was allocated an alphabetical suffix, e.g. 22a – the Open Sports Car, and could be purchased either individually or as part of the set.

In April 1934 the Modelled Miniatures series, also known briefly as 'Meccano Miniatures', was renamed 'Dinky Toys'. In the space of just five years these models, which had begun as mere railway accessories,

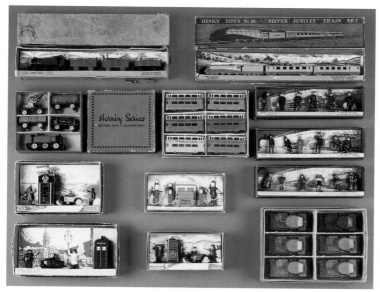

Left: *Pre-war sets and series. The train sets (top left) and the tank (22f) (bottom right) were made of lead. Also shown are the Silver Jubilee Train (16); Passengers and Station Staff; the AA, RAC, Police and Petrol Pump sets, together with a box of trams.*

Below: *A page from the 'Meccano Magazine' issue dated May 1934, showing many of the new Dinky Toy sets and series.*

had become collectable in their own right and, judging by contemporary comments, extremely popular. Between April and December many new sets and individual items were announced, so that by Christmas 1934 there was an amazing total of more than one hundred items in the toyshops, ranging from a pig or a sheep at twopence each or a tank (No. 22f) at one shilling to a complete set of eight cars, the 24 series, costing six shillings and sixpence. The December 1934 edition of the *Meccano Magazine* explained: 'We were repeatedly asked for other miniatures, mainly of motor cars, aeroplanes and ships, and finally it was decided to introduce a comprehensive series of models under the general title of Dinky Toys.' After describing the train sets, commercial vehicles and racing cars, the article went on: 'Another very attractive vehicle is the "Holland Coachcraft" van (No. 31). This is a model of one of the most modernistic commercial vehicles now on the road.' It was to

Famous Liners, series 51. (Left, from top) 51c Rex; 51f Queen of Bermuda; 51d Empress of Britain. (Right, from top) 51b Europa; 51e Strathaird; 51g Britannic. In pre-war boxed set, dated October 1934.

be 'ready shortly'. Also introduced in late 1934 were six new aeroplanes (60a to 60f) and seventeen ships, both British naval vessels and ocean liners. So the range expanded to one hundred and fifty by June 1935 and to two hundred by February 1936.

New releases continued to arrive regularly so that between June 1935 and December 1938 another hundred and fifty new items had been added to the catalogue, an average of almost four each month.

This was an extraordinary production period for Dinky Toys, the like of which the company would never experience again. Many attractive sets or series were advertised during these pre-war years. A 'series' consisted of similar models such as series 25, the commercial vehicle series (i.e. 25a through to 25y, which totalled eighteen items as not all suffix letters were used), and a 'set' consisted of a number of related models, packaged in one box and promoted as a 'gift set', e.g. Set No. 12, representing six Royal Mail items – a highly sought-after boxed set.

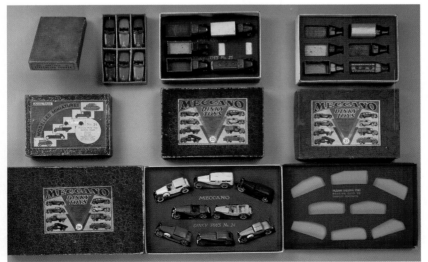

Valuable pre-war boxed sets. Sets containing the 24 series of cars and the 25 series of wagons together with a trade box of six Streamline Tourers (22g) and an early Modelled Miniatures box for the 24 series.

23 series of Racing Cars. (Centre rear, on pre-war 23 Racing Car box) 23a Racing Cars (three). (Front, left to right) 23b Hotchkiss; 23d Auto-Union; 23p MG Magnette; 23e Speed of the Wind.

The simplest method of describing the new models is in the order of their series number although each series was not actually introduced chronologically. More comprehensive descriptions of the toys can be found in the books listed under 'Further reading' at the end of this book. See also the simplified numbering table.

The first group was the 22 set/series in 1933 (already described), followed in 1934 by the first of the 23 series – a colourful range of racing cars that continued until 1953. The 24 series comprised seven cars and an ambulance, this last item at that stage not fitting conveniently into any other series. Commercial vehicles formed the 25 series, lasting until 1954. 26 and 27 were one-offs, a railcar and tramcar respectively. These models were produced for only a short period, possibly because their smaller scale made them incompatible with other larger and more expansive ranges. The 28 series of small delivery vans was an important group with well over seventy delightful vehicles painted in many colours and advertising contemporary products such as Seccotine, Marsh's Sausages, Wakefield Oil, Atco Mowers, Virol and Ovaltine. Nowadays these little vans, which cost a mere sixpence to buy when first released, are very expensive to acquire.

Nineteen of the total of seventy-five 28 series pre-war vans with advertising, including Fry's, Hovis, Ecko and the extremely rare Bentalls van, which sold in October 1994 for what was then a world record for a Dinky Toy, £12,650.

A rare 36 series boxed set, containing six cars with figures, produced about 1938. Also shown is the original packaging material.

Another significant group was the 29 series of buses, always popular with children. All these series (23 to 29) commenced production in 1934, although it would be some twenty years before the last models in the series joined the earlier products.

In June 1935 another series, 30, appeared, starting with four cars but then surprisingly changing to commercial vehicles from the fifth model onwards. This was also a large series, comprising sixteen castings. As always with Dinky Toys, many different colour combinations were applied. 31 and 32 were one-offs; 31, the Holland Coachcraft van, has already been mentioned. Its basic casting was also used, with appropriate side windows, as a bus that appeared in the 29 series. Later 31 series vans, based on a Trojan, appeared after the Second World War. 32 was a Chrysler Airflow.

The 33 series was another colourful range, this time of articulated vans, mainly in the liveries of railway companies such as that of the Great Western Railway, splendidly decorated in brown and cream, with appropriate motifs. The last new series in 1935 was the three-model 34 group: 34a, a short-lived Air Service Car, has since suffered from metal fatigue and thus mint examples are very rare; 34b and 34c were later additions.

In 1936 the 35 series began, comprising very small and basic Dublo-style (00 gauge, 1:72 scale) cars, followed in 1938 by a significant range of six luxury British cars and a taxi, the 36 series, together with the 37 series, small-scale motorcycles. Just before the war two highly sought-after series, 38 and 39, were introduced. Fortunately for collectors, these were reissued after the war. The 38 group was six British sports cars; 39 was six American cars.

The 40 series did not appear until 1947 and the 41 series was never issued. This was a rare occurrence and gave rise to speculation within the toy-collecting community.

Series 42, 43 and 44 were not only series but also sets representing

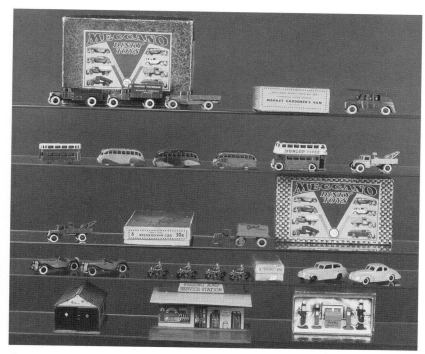

A pre-war miscellany. 25 series wagons, 29 series buses, early American 39 series cars, the Garage, Filling Station and Petrol Pumps are some of the items illustrated.

25 series wagons. Twenty-four different wagons including some rare Petrol Wagons, e.g. Redline-Glico and Pool; Covered Wagons in Carter Paterson and Meccano liveries together with other models from the series.

Post-war 29 series single-deck buses. 29b Streamline Bus (left); 29e Half Cab Coach (two) (foreground); 29f Observation Coach (two) (right); 29g Luxury Coach (three) (middle); 29h Duple Roadmaster (four) (back row).

Eight members of the 36 series. (Bottom row from left) 36b Bentley (blue); 36b Bentley (green); 36c Humber Vogue; 36d Rover. (Top row from left) 36e British Salmson (red); 36f British Salmson (grey); 36f British Salmson (green); 36g Taxi.

39 series. On trade box: 39f Studebaker State Commander (left); 39a Packard Super 8 Sedan (two, second left and far right); 39b Oldsmobile Six Sedan (second right). Foreground: (left) 39e Chrysler Royal; (right) 39d Buick Viceroy.

16

Pre-war military models: 151b Six-wheel Transport Wagon (right); 152b Reconnaissance Car (left); 160 Army Personnel (front); 161b Mobile Anti-aircraft Gun, pre-war and post-war versions (centre back); 151a Medium Tank (front left); 151c Cooker Trailer (right).

the police, the Royal Automobile Club and the Automobile Association respectively. All three appeared in 1935 or 1936.

Series 45 to 49 were allocated from 1935 to non-wheeled items such as a garage, road signs, a filling station and petrol pumps.

The 50 series onwards were allocated to ships and 60 onwards to aeroplanes, consisting of over forty different models.

Dolls' house furniture was numbered from 100, and from 1937 series numbers from 150 to 160 were allocated to military items. The pre-war junior wargamer had enough armoured toys, comprising over twenty individual items and many sets, to create his own miniature British khaki army. By 1939 real war was threatening, and just a handful of military models were released in 1940 and 1941 before the Binns Road factory ceased production.

A fascinating diversion occurred in October 1940, when the directors launched an appeal to raise funds to purchase an RAF Spitfire aeroplane. A miniature Spitfire pendant was sold for two shillings and sixpence and within a month twenty-six thousand models had been

Eight pre-war aeroplanes. (Clockwise from front left) 60n Fairy Battle Bomber; 62g Boeing Flying Fortress; 62m Airspeed Envoy (yellow box); 60h Singapore Flying Boat (blue box); 62p Armstrong Whitworth Ensign. (Centre, left to right) 62a Spitfire Fund (red); 60g DH Comet (gold).

Three rare pre-war aeroplanes: 63 Mayo Composite Aircraft (left); 68a Armstrong Whitworth Ensign Bomber (front right); 67a Junkers JU 89 Heavy Bomber (back right); with gliding game instructions and pre-war boxes.

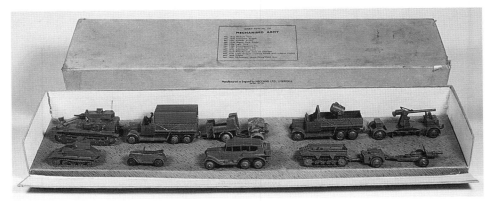

Mechanised Army set No. 156 consisting of military vehicles, including 161a Searchlight Lorry and 152c Austin Seven. Pre-war box dated January 1940.

sold, raising £3250 towards the Spitfire Fund. A boxed model is extremely rare today.

This was the end of the most prolific production period in the history of Dinky Toys. Models manufactured between 1931 and 1941 are highly collectable because many Dinky Toys were destroyed or discarded during the Second World War. The government encouraged children to recycle their metal toys, so that the scrap material could be used to produce aeroplanes and tanks. During the war, the Binns Road factory turned to essential munition manufacturing, utilising their diecasting machinery.

A Dinky Toy for Christmas. Shortages of Dinky Toys, especially during wartime, created limited supplies and queues at toyshops. This photograph shows two young boys and their mother outside a toyshop in Thetford, Norfolk.

'THE ONES *WITHOUT* WINDOWS'
(1946–58)

In September 1943 the government prohibited the sale of metal toys, and it was not until the end of hostilities that the Meccano factory in Liverpool recommenced production of Dinky Toys. It was announced in the December 1945 *Meccano Magazine* that the company would be releasing Meccano sets and Dinky Toys, but the first new Dinky Toy did not appear until April 1946. Like the last pre-war Dinky Toy, the Searchlight Lorry (22s), introduced some six years earlier, the first post-war toy, the US Jeep, was also a military vehicle. Between 1939 and 1947 toy collectors had to be very patient since only a very few toys were issued to shops, mainly for Christmas, and then more often only to large stores such as Gamages. Nowadays many older people remember queuing for hours at Christmas during the war, hoping for just one Dinky Toy for their children.

Gradually, however, production returned to normal, and, as well as the US Military Jeep (153a), three civilian sports cars arrived later in 1946. These were a follow-on from pre-war days, when the 38 series, consisting of six sports cars, had been announced in June 1939 but production had been interrupted by the war. This series lasted only until 1950; the final three models were the Lagonda (38c), the SS Jaguar (38f) and the Armstrong Siddeley (38e).

War stops play. The government announcement prohibiting the sale of toys appeared on 30th September 1943, the month the author was born.

Ten members of the 38 series. (Front, from left) 38a Frazer-Nash BMW (grey); 38f SS Jaguar (blue); 38f SS Jaguar (red); 38d Alvis (brown); 38b Sunbeam-Talbot (yellow); 38d Alvis (green); 38e Armstrong Siddeley (green). (Back) 38c Lagonda (three) on a post-war trade box.

Before the war it had been planned that 38e would be the Triumph Dolomite, but, although this reached the drawing board, it did not go into production.

Post-war versions of the 39 series, the six American cars, also appeared at this time, all with slight variations from their pre-war counterparts. These differences occurred on most of the Dinky Toy reissues of pre-war releases, which had a standard post-war road wheel with a ridge, distinguishing it from the plain 'fatter' pre-war version. The colours were often more drab and 'utilitarian' compared to the brighter paintwork of the 1930s. Some pre-war baseplates were left unpainted with just a clear varnish and, particularly immediately before 1940, could often be recycled from tinplate Hornby Train offcuts, whereas post-war baseplates were painted black. Steering wheels and the Perspex windscreens on the sports cars were also slightly altered. These are just some of the distinctions between pre-war and post-war Dinky Toys. The American car series and the sports cars were the first complete series to name the car on which each model was based individually on the baseplate. This arrangement continued, with a few minor exceptions, until the closure of the factory in 1979.

Many other pre-war series were reintroduced during the late 1940s, all easily distinguishable from the pre-war versions, and this production continued into the 1950s until sufficient new models had been introduced to replace what by then had become fairly ancient-looking vehicles. One whole set, the 25 series trucks, originally introduced in 1934

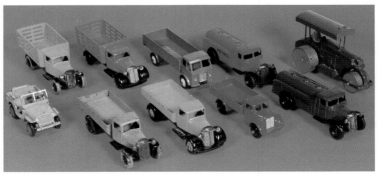

Commercial vehicles from series 22 and 25. (From left) 25j US Jeep (Civilian); 25a/e/f wagons (four); 25r Forward Control Lorry (rear-middle); 22c Motor Truck (front-middle); 25d Petrol Tank Wagons (two); 25p Aveling Barford Roller.

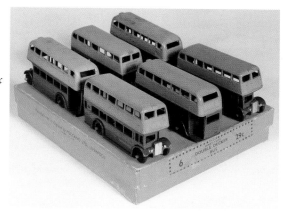

Six Double Decker Buses (29c), all with AEC radiators, produced in the immediate post-war years. These colour variations of green/grey and green/light green are unusual. The pre-war trade box is dated May 1939.

(and probably based on actual 1920s vehicles), was eventually replaced from 1950 onwards by modern equivalents as in the following table:

original	*replacement*	*date*
25a Wagon	30j Austin Wagon	June 1950
25b Covered Wagon	30s Austin Covered Wagon	September 1950
25c Flat Truck	30r Fordson Thames Flat Truck	February 1951
25d Petrol Tank Wagon	30p Petrol Tanker (Studebaker)	May 1950
25e Tipping Wagon	30m Rear Tipping Wagon (Dodge)	August 1950
25f Market Gardener's Van	30n Farm Produce Wagon (Dodge)	May 1950
25g Trailer	25g Trailer (revised)	(February 1951)

Before the war the small Trailer (25g) matched the colours of the Flat Truck (25c); this was repeated from 1951 with the Fordson Thames Flat Truck and the Trailer, although they were not sold as a set, as the former pair had been. About one hundred individual pre-war models, including aeroplanes, trucks and at least seventy cars, were reissued between 1946 and 1951 and a few managed to survive, although much modified, through to the 1954–5 'renumbering period' (more of which later). As new models were introduced, the pre-war reissues were gradually replaced.

Models that were popular enough for Meccano to reissue after the war were:

original number	*model*	*new number*	*pre-war*	*post-war*	*production run* (years)*
23e	Speed of the Wind	221	1936–41	1946–57	17
25g	Small Trailer	429	1935–40	1946–63	24
25h	Fire Engine	250	1936–40	1948–62	20
29c	Double Decker Bus	290	1938–41	1946–63	21
33a/33w	Mechanical Horse	415	1935–40	1947–59	19
34c/280	Bedford Van	492	1939–41	1948–57	12
35b	Small Racer	200	1936–40	1946–57	17
63b	Sea Plane	700	1939–41	1946–57	14

* excluding war years; all dates approximate.

It would be inconceivable for a toy today to survive a production run of twenty-four years! There are about twenty variations, including colour differences, for the Trailer, and even more for the Double Decker

Post-war 25 series Bedfords. (Front row, left to right) 25v Refuse Wagon (early and later versions); 25w Bedford Truck; 25m Tipper (early, with black wheels). (Back row, left to right) 25wm Military Truck; 25m Tipper (two later versions); 25w Bedford Truck (early version).

Bus. This was probably the most popular Dinky Toy ever: according to a former employee, it 'became one of the biggest-selling toys, both at home and overseas, of all time'.

Following the many reissues of the late 1940s, Dinky Toy production was now returning to normal, and more brand-new items were being announced to reflect contemporary road transport. A very significant, entirely new range was introduced in 1947: Dinky Supertoys. At first Foden and Guy lorries were represented, together with a Shetland Flying Boat, but these were merely the first of hundreds of larger attractive commercial vehicles. However, the company was still affected by military conflicts since at this time the war in Korea had caused a shortage of materials, so that in 1951 manufacture was again scaled back with only ten new issues, well below Meccano's pre-war production rates. When the crisis was over, dozens of significant models were introduced during the 1950s and these have been important in today's toy-collecting nostalgia.

Whole series, sets and groups were produced, providing Dinky Toys with a huge proportion of the toy-buying market. These included:

● 1950s popular saloon cars, including the Hillman Minx, the Rover 75 and the Austin Somerset (in the 40 and 140 series).

Supertoys Fodens. (Left, front and back) 502 Flat Truck (two). (Right, front and back) 504 Tanker (two). (Back centre left) 505 Flat Truck with Chains. (Back centre right) 504 Mobilgas Tanker. Note the different types of boxes.

Above: *40 series British cars. (Front, left to right) 40a Riley (three); 40b Triumph; 40d Austin Devon; 40e Standard Vanguard (two). (Back, left to right) 40f Hillman Minx (two); 40g Morris Oxford (two); 40h Austin Taxi (two); 40j Austin Somerset (two).*

The 100 series of racing sports cars: (from left) Aston Martin, Austin Healey, Aston Martin, Austin Healey, MG Midget, Triumph TR2, Sunbeam Alpine, Bristol 450, MG Midget, Triumph TR2; supplied with or without racing numbers.

● A very attractive series of racing cars comprising a Ferrari, an Alfa Romeo, a Maserati and others. These were initially a continuation of the pre-war 23 series of racing cars.

● Sports cars complemented the above two groups; once again a colourful range of twenty contemporary cars, this time all British, including famous marques such as MG, Austin Healey and Aston Martin.

● Farm machinery was not ignored, the company possibly hoping to attract girls to what was a male-dominated hobby. Tractors, hay rakes and Land-Rovers formed part of this range.

● Very popular and with considerable play value were lorries, wagons,

Farm equipment: the 27 series. 27a Massey-Harris Tractor; 27b Harvest Trailer; 27f Estate Car; 27g Motocart; 27j Triple Gang Mower; 27d Land-Rover; 27m Land-Rover Trailer and infiltrator; 25y Universal Jeep (announced as 27y in the 'Meccano Magazine' of October 1952).

23

Guy vans. All are numbered 514, which was unusual, although internally the company was treating them as 514 (Slumberland); 515 (Lyons); 516 (Weetabix); and 517 (Spratts). The Spratts van was renumbered 917 in 1954.

Right: 31 series Trojan vans. 31a (450) Esso (front); 31c (452) Chivers (right). (On the Esso trade box, from the back) 31d (453) Oxo; 455 Brooke Bond Tea; 454 Cydrax; 31b (451) Dunlop, not illustrated.

trucks and transport equipment. Dinky Toys produced wide and varied ranges covering general haulage, delivery vehicles, petrol and oil tankers and earth-moving machinery as well as emergency vehicles such as ambulances, fire engines and police cars.

● Buses, always popular, were represented by miniature versions of the actual road vehicles.

These ranges, which were being introduced at the rate of two models per month on average, provided children with a huge selection, and the market was insatiable. As always, Dinky Toys made the most of their costly investment in machinery, workforce, packaging and marketing by producing not only many colour variations of most models but also, in the case of vans and tankers, toys with contemporary advertising. The Guy and Trojan vans introduced from 1949 and 1951 respectively are good examples of this practice; six Guys and six Trojans (identical castings of each) were issued, all in different attractive liveries. As with all the vans of the 1950s, these items are particularly collectable today.

Below: Rare post-war sets. Five gift sets from the 1950s and 1960s, including Racing Cars, Sports Cars, Post Office Vans and the Bedford Car Transporter, complete with four cars.

Fire engines. (Left and centre) Two Commer fire engines (955), early and later (with windows) versions. (Front and right) Turntable Fire Escape, Bedford and Berliet Versions (956). (Back) A Fire Service Gift Set (957).

Pre-war and post-war military sets. (Front) No. 161 Mobile Anti-Aircraft Unit in a pre-war box dated November 1939. (Back) No. 699 Military Vehicles gift set, introduced 1955.

Meccano also used their initiative, usually at Christmas, in packaging the groups into sets, so that parents could purchase sets of racing cars, passenger cars or farm equipment in large boxes for that special occasion.

Having neglected the military scene for several years, Dinky Toys revived a vast new range of models, which were to be one of the most successful groups of toys ever produced by the company. Even today, hoards of these army vehicles appear at collectors' fairs and auctions, reflecting the production of millions of toys throughout the 1950s.

In 1954 what was to become a series of over thirty military vehicles, all to the same scale of 1:60 and included in a new numerical list between 600 and 699, was begun. The detail on these models was very accurate, appearing to be much superior to that on other toys being produced at the time. This may have been due to close co-operation with Army contacts, or it may have been that a separate department was set up to produce the models in view of the wide range.

Also in 1954 there were complicated changes to the Dinky Toys numbering system. A system of numbers and suffix letters had been used for the smaller toys (larger toys were an exception) since the first Modelled Miniature 1a in 1931, but now this method was abandoned in favour of three-digit numbers, in the range 001 to 999. A few models,

Eight Land-Rovers and three Trailers, all different, produced from 1950 to 1971. Versions were available in three main body colours, green, orange and red, with or without metal or plastic drivers. Wheels were metal or plastic, and there was a variety of interior colours.

Austin Atlantic (140a and 106) variations, with different individual boxes and an early version of the trade box. There are at least twelve versions of the Atlantic.

Left: *Rare post-war Farm Tractor and Hay Rake set, No. 27ak, with original box, packaging and 'tested' label; introduced in 1953; renumbered 310 in 1954. Dinky Toys were consistent in their application of suffix letters. On the box, as shown here, where all the lettering is upper-case, the model number is printed in capitals: 27AK. Where the type is lower-case, for example in a 'Meccano Magazine' advertisement, it would be printed 27ak.*

after 1971, had four-digit numbers ranging from 1001 to 1050 (Action Kits), and three Ford Capris, which were non-standard items, were numbered 2162, 2214 and 2253. Some of the larger vehicles had already been allocated numbers in this range. For example, the Dinky Supertoys, so-called for their extra size and cost, had been numbered between 501 and 599 from 1947, the military vehicles had been allocated numbers from 601 to 699, and the aeroplanes those from 700 to 749.

The reasons for the change included the increase in the range of the toys offered for sale, the clumsiness of the existing system, which ran out of suffix letters for a large series, and the problems caused when letters were confused with numbers (such as I for 1, b

'Meccano Magazine', March 1954: an advertisement for Dinky Toys showing clearly the old and the new model numbers. Also shown are lengths and prices.

Later additions to the 30 series (commenced 1935): 30v NCB Electric Dairy Van, in three different liveries, and 30w Electric Articulated Lorry in British Railways livery; introduced in 1949 and 1953 respectively.

Left: *Post-war aeroplanes. (Clockwise from left) 70a Avro York Air Liner; 70c Viking Air Liner in silver and grey; 70b Hawker Tempest Fighter; 70f Shooting Star Fighter. (From centre to front) 735 Gloster Javelin Fighter; 736 Hawker Hunter Fighter; 734 Supermarine Swift Fighter.*

Right: *Road repair and maintenance vehicles. (Front) Snow Plough (two versions) (958). (Back row from left) Muir-Hill Dumper Truck (two versions – the right-hand one is an Indian version by Nicky Toys) (962); Albion Cement Mixer (960); Blaw-Knox Heavy Tractor (963).*

Three larger passenger aircraft. Two D H Comets (left and right), 999 and 702, registration numbers G-ALYX and G-ALYV respectively. (Centre) 701 Shetland Flying Boat, from 1948.

for 6 and O for zero), but most important was the introduction at Meccano of up-to-date new office machinery that utilised a forerunner of the modern computer, the Power-Samas system. This gave Meccano the opportunity of placing the majority of toys in separate ranges, for example:

001– 099	Dublo toys (from 1957) and tyres
100–199	Convertibles and saloon cars
200–249	Racing and sports cars
250–299	Emergency and public service vehicles
300–399	Farm equipment
400–499	Commercial vehicles
500–599	Dinky Supertoys, later French-made cars (see below)
600–699	Military vehicles
700–749	Aeroplanes
750–799	Accessories and non-wheeled items
800–899	French-made commercial vehicles
900–999	Dinky Supertoys (larger models).

Up to 1954 the range 500–599 had been Dinky Supertoys. These were then mostly renumbered in the range 900–999, as above, with the 500–599 numbers being allocated to Dinky Toys cars made in France. (Parts of these ranges were available in limited quantities in the United Kingdom.)

This revised numbering system continued almost unchanged, with minor exceptions and additions, until 1980. It must have been much easier for the company, its agents and dealers to operate, although not quite as fascinating for the avid Dinky Toy collector.

Dinky Supertoys had disappeared from the company's catalogues for a couple of years, possibly owing to a metal shortage following the Korean War, but in June 1955 one of the first entirely new models, apart from those being renumbered from the 500 series to the 900s, was a splendid Foden tanker. This eight-wheeled wagon was authentically painted in the red, white and blue of the Regent oil company. 1955 was a productive year for new issues, with toys appearing in several different categories – small cars, a new sports-car range, more military vehicles, small and large vans and Supertoys. This would be the last year of Dinky Toy predominance in the diecast toy world. Although it would not become apparent for some years, 1956 was the beginning of the end for Dinky Toys. By that date the toys had been available for twenty-five years and had had a virtual monopoly, particularly in Great Britain. Competition would now start to erode sales, but Dinky Toys would be fighting back for some years yet.

Matchbox Toys had been marketed seriously since their success with the Coronation Coach in 1953, and sales of their small cars were growing.

The 900 series of Fodens and Leylands. (Back row from left) 901 Foden 8-Wheel Wagon; 902 Foden Flat Truck; 905 Foden Flat with Chains (two); 941 Foden Mobilgas Tanker. (Front) 934 Leyland Octopus Wagon (two).

Dinky and Matchbox were joined in 1956 by a new competitor, Corgi Toys. This company had developed from a long-established toy company that until then had traded under the uninspiring name of Mettoy. By choosing a catchy new name with royal associations, the new Welsh company did not take long to establish itself and to compete head to head with Dinky Toys. Corgi Toys were very similar in concept to Dinky Toys: they were the familiar size and scale, depicting current British cars and trucks; even the boxes, apart from the colour, were almost identical in size, shape and design. But there were two main differences: Corgi, in order to be one step ahead, included clear plastic windows in all its models from the beginning; and a selection of their range included toys with a 'push and go' mechanism – never a feature of Dinky Toys. Corgi Toys discontinued this mechanism a few years later, as it proved unpopular with collectors. So similar were the castings from the two factories at that time that if a Corgi Toy were taken apart and had Dinky Toy wheels added and the plastic windows removed it could appear to be a new issue from Dinky. Indeed in 1956 both Dinky and Corgi issued versions of a large Ford saloon that would look very similar to the uninitiated. However, Dinky Toys were not then to know whether Corgi would be a mere flash in the pan or would prove to be more enduring, but Corgi outlasted Dinky by many years.

1956 was a productive year for Meccano, when many new models were issued, including small cars and vans, military vehicles, amongst

Below left: 'Meccano Magazine', August 1955: a photograph of a mechanical display of the New Jersey Turnpike near New York. Over 150 Dinky Toys were on display.

Below right: 'Meccano Magazine', October 1955: the heyday of Dinky Toy popularity when often three new models were introduced simultaneously in a month. The author was given the Dump Truck for his twelfth birthday. It was his last childhood toy.

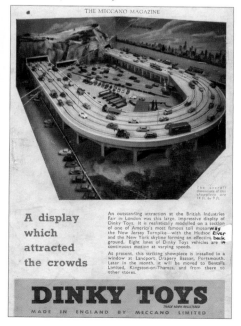

Dublo series. 061 Ford Prefect to 078 Trailer. Fifteen models produced from 1957 to 1966.

them the spectacular Thornycroft Mighty Antar tank transporter complete with a Centurion tank, and other Supertoys. Perhaps to compete with Corgi, many of the older small cars, such as the Rover 75, the Morris Oxford and the Ford Fordor, were repainted in two-tone colour schemes, which gave them an extended life; the majority, however, lasted only until 1960. As usual, Meccano were extracting the maximum profit from their expensive machinery.

Another countermeasure against increasing competition was the introduction in 1957 of the Dinky Toys Club. This new organisation, advertised through the *Meccano Magazine,* was a natural development of previous Hornby initiatives for collectors. The first, the Meccano Guild, had been introduced in 1918, and a similar club for Hornby Train collectors was started in 1928. Members received a badge and a scroll. Thousands of children signed up, and their collections were featured regularly in the *Meccano Magazine.*

In 1957 there were further additions to recently introduced series, enabling fleets to be extended. These included small tankers, such as the 'National Benzole'; small vans, such as the Trojan 'Cydrax' and the Morris 'Capstan'; large vans, such as the Guy 'Golden Shred'; yet more military vehicles; and sports cars in touring finish, i.e. without racing numbers. Just before the end of the year an important yet short-lived and limited new series was announced. This was the Dublo-scale (00) group of cars, vans and trucks. Although totalling only fifteen, they are nowadays highly collectable both by Dinky Toy and Hornby Train devotees. Matchbox had been manufacturing small-scale toys since 1953, and this was Dinky Toys' response, but they were rather late on the scene and were never as popular as their rivals, hence their early demise from the catalogues by 1967. Their scarcity today leads collectors to believe that sales were not buoyant and that Dinky Toys were beginning to feel the pressure from competitors.

Eventually, in 1958, two years after Corgi Toys had introduced plastic windows, Dinky Toys added these features gradually to both new and existing models. The first Dinky Toy with plastic windows was the Austin A105 Saloon (176), introduced in April 1958, followed by several other new British, European and American cars during that year. Not all new issues, however, were supplied with windows; a few were launched without this feature but later had them added if the model lasted long enough in production. Examples of this were the Guy Warrior lorries (431/2/920).

Dinky Toys with windows. (Front row, from left) The first with windows, Austin A105 (176) (two); simultaneous release, Triumph Herald (189) (two); Rolls-Royce (150). (Middle row, from left) Austin 1800 (171); Vauxhall Cresta (164); Hillman Minx (175) (two). (Back row, from left) Four caravans: 188; 190 (without windows); 188; 190 (without windows).

American sedans from 1958 to 1962. (Left-hand row, from top) Studebaker President; Packard Clipper; Nash Rambler; Cadillac 62. (Middle row, from top) Studebaker President; Hudson Hornet; Nash Rambler; Cadillac 62. (Right-hand row, from top) Ford Fairlane (three); Hudson Hornet.

THE FINAL YEARS (1959–79)

Because of the increasing competition from various manufacturers, 1958 had been the crucial turning point for Dinky Toys with the introduction of more realism such as windows and treaded tyres. From 1959, the innovations continued apace; of the many new ideas, some were original but several were copied from their rivals.

In the years after the Second World War consumers were eager to obtain any type of toy, as long as it was affordable, but as the western world became more prosperous the public was given more choice. Thus, whatever the industry, the company that produced something completely new or different was able to steal a march on its competitors. So it was in the toy trade, and throughout the 1960s Dinky Toy collectors saw more changes than had taken place during the previous thirty years.

From 1959 there was a plethora of American, continental and British export-type cars, including Packards, Studebakers, De Sotos, Plymouths and Dodges from the United States, Mercedes and Volkswagens from Germany and Rolls-Royces, Bentleys and Triumphs from Britain. British children were unfamiliar with American automobile names and shapes, but the long sleek duo-tone styling, wrap-round windows and tail fins of American cars gave the impression that they came from another planet. Their blatant attractiveness would appeal more than their dull

European cars. (Top row, from left) Volkswagen (181) (three); Mercedes-Benz 250SE (160); Alfa Romeo 1900 (185); Saab 96 (156). (Front row, from left) Volkswagen 1500 (144); Opel Commodore (179); BMW 2000 (157); Opel Kapitan (177); Citroën Dyane (149).

British counterparts, such as a plain brown diminutive Austin A30. Dinky Toys at this time were heavily committed to the export drive and were seeking increased sales in the United States, a huge and potentially more prosperous market, so the concentration on American-based models was a sound financial strategy. Other models of American vehicles made in this period include several police cars, the Wayne School Bus in yellow and the McLeans Tractor-Trailer Unit.

These new American cars introduced two new features, one of which would stay with the toys for at least a further ten years. After thirty years of plain diecast wheels, chromed dished wheels and white tyres added realism to these popular toys.

In 1959 Dinky Toys produced the first new model of a Rolls-Royce since the 1930s, the Silver Wraith. This model, appealing to both home and overseas markets, set new trends. It was the longest British Dinky Toy car, at 12 cm (4³/₄ inches), and looked very attractive in two-tone grey, featuring the new plated wheels but with more traditional black tyres. Added attractions were a plated radiator grille, complete with the Spirit of Ecstasy mascot, plated bumpers and independent suspension, described in the February 1959 edition of the *Meccano Magazine* as 'a special new development, exclusive to Dinky Toys'. All this resulted in an appealing toy, but the price, at five shillings and sixpence (including tax), made the Rolls-Royce the most expensive Dinky Toy car yet, no doubt reflecting its real-life counterpart, but also to cover the enormous manufacturing costs, which would continue to rise over the coming years. Prices would generally increase during the next few years. The Silver Wraith was extremely popular, with many toys still in existence today, and was the forerunner of many more Rolls-Royce and Bentley models. A basic saloon car of 1958, such as the Rover 75 or Ford Zephyr, cost three shillings, but only three years later saloon cars would be selling at about five shillings. Inflation was making itself felt in Britain.

In May 1959 the Dinky Toy model of the Triumph Herald was

released at the same time as the actual car – the first time this had happened. The publicity announced that 'the model, based on the maker's own blue-prints, faithfully reflects the sophisticated lines of this ... saloon'. It was quite a coup. The popular series of BBC and ABC television outside-broadcast vehicles also commenced in May 1959 and are much sought after today. Later in the year French Dinky Toys began to be imported into the United Kingdom. This had previously occurred before the war, and the trend was to continue until the factory closure.

The BBC-TV Vehicles Set: (front) Mobile Control Room (967); (back left) Roving Eye Vehicle (968); (centre) Extending Mast Vehicle (969).

Although not entirely new in concept, commercial vehicles featured further sophisticated mechanical detailing, such as a missile launcher, a pallet van with a movable platform and what is now known as a skip truck. By 1960 more new features included interiors (seats and steering wheels) in an Atlas minibus and 'fingertip steering' together with an interior for the Jaguar 3.4 litre saloon. Again Dinky Toys were beaten by their arch-rivals, Corgi, who had introduced passenger compartments some months earlier.

In 1961 the *Meccano Magazine* changed to a larger format, similar to that used before the war. Illustrations of new Dinky Toys were therefore increased in size, occasionally with more details. A fascinating article appeared in the May 1961 edition of the magazine describing how the Austin Seven Countryman was made and, although production figures have never been published, it was stated that 'Meccano Limited are able to put millions of models on to the market every year'. The *Meccano Magazine* did not remain much longer in Meccano's ownership, and in 1964 it was transferred to another publisher, leaving the Binns Road factory to concentrate on toy production. Faced with increasing competition not only from other toy magazines but also from the teenage and television markets, the magazine's circulation had been falling.

Model production continued on similar lines, with further American sedans, an occasional aeroplane, at least fifteen more imports from the French Dinky factory in Paris and an all-new Leyland Atlantean bus. In October 1962 there was another first. The MGB Sports Car, still popular today, was the first Dinky Toy made with opening doors. It also

Supertoys of the late 1950s. (Left to right) 918 Guy Ever Ready; 920 Guy Heinz; 922 Bedford Lorry (a Dinky Toy not a Supertoy); 923 Bedford Heinz; 930 Bedford Dinky Toys.

(Top row) Three American 39 series cars destined for export. The remaining models were issued mainly at the end of their respective production runs and often appeared in unusual colour combinations which were different from the initial issues. For example, the Triumph 1800 (second row, left) was painted black. Also shown is a toy dealer's metal sign.

contained most of the other innovations introduced since windows appeared in 1958: a plastic windscreen, interior details, plated wheels, fingertip (now called 'Prestomatic') steering and suspension. Like the Triumph Herald, it was introduced at the same time as the actual car, another scoop for Meccano.

By 1963 competition was intense. In the United Kingdom Corgi Toys were producing a similar range to Dinky Toys. Not only were the scale, size and material of the models almost identical, so that toys could be interchanged on layouts, but Corgi had followed Dinky by introducing a series of larger, more expensive models called Corgi Major Toys. Major Toys competed directly with Dinky Supertoys, which had been introduced in 1947, featuring Foden and Guy trucks. From the late 1950s Dinky Toys had lost their dominance in this market. At the cheaper end of the market, Matchbox toys were gradually eroding Meccano's supremacy. From the 1950s their cheap but very attractive series were beginning to establish a presence both in Britain and in the more important export markets. Their very successful series of innovative Yesteryear cars and vans diluted Dinky sales in the mid-range trade. Tri-ang, a minor competitor since the 1930s and owned by Lines Bros, had been producing toys in tinplate but after the war manufactured virtually all of its products using plastic. Their output was not very popular and rather crude compared to the diecast products. Not surprisingly, Lines Bros decided to produce their own diecast toys, called Spot-On, made in Northern Ireland. Although not produced in the same quantity as Dinky Toys, these models too affected Meccano sales. Abroad, Meccano competed against not only their British rivals but Solido in France, Tekno in Denmark, Mercury in Italy, Märklin in Germany, Tootsietoy in the United States and Japanese toys.

Dinky Toys had set themselves an almost impossible target of at least two new models each month. When they held a large proportion of the

Fire, ambulance and public service vehicles. 250 to 261, together with a rare later trade pack of six for the Royal Mail Van (260).

toy market and production was successful, this was possible, but as the pressure increased they had to search for other ideas. For many years the same casting had been utilised over and over again, particularly for vans with different advertising, so the company was not inexperienced in adaptation. Thus in the late 1950s and early 1960s many models were reissued in different liveries such as police and fire cars or taxis and large expensive sets containing individual items helped to ensure the profit margins remained high. However, all this activity, together with several new models and features, did not help the company, which by the end of 1963 was suffering from financial losses.

Just before this major financial crisis, Meccano introduced further toys with even more new features. Following opening doors, Dinky Toys appeared in 1962 and 1963 with opening windows (the Rolls-Royce Phantom V), opening boot with luggage (the Jaguar Mark 10), an ambulance with a flashing light (the first of several), opening bonnet with a detailed engine (the Morris 1100 Saloon – another simultaneous launch with the actual road car), and a new series of Formula 1 racing cars, including the famous Ferrari, Lotus and Cooper.

In the final months of the Meccano ownership of Dinky Toys there were several fascinating new models. Cars included the Ford Cortina with reclining seats, an American Plymouth Convertible with a removable soft-top, and the Triumph Spitfire (yet another simultaneous issue) with the first 'lady driver'. Many toys now included drivers or personnel to add reality. Two of the final models for 1963 were another Triumph (in more ways than one!) and an excavator. The Triumph 2000 appeared on Dinky roads well before its full-sized brother, and the Ruston-Bucyrus Excavator was a masterpiece of model engineering. At twenty-seven shillings and sixpence, it was one of the most expensive British Dinky Toys then available, which is why it is so rare today. Meccano, at

Racing and rally cars including Ferrari, BRM, Lotus, Matra, Ford GT, Fiat, Alfa Romeo, Hillman Imp, Ford Cortina and McLaren.

35

Bedford TK Trucks and a Commer: the earlier Bedford Top Rank Breakdown Truck with the later Auto Services Truck; two Tipper trucks and an Articulated Convertible Commer from 1963 and 1964.

least, went out with a bang, launching what are today two highly sought-after models.

In January 1964 Meccano Ltd had reached the point where it could not carry on in business without additional financial support, so the company was taken over by one of its rivals, Lines Bros, the manufacturers of Tri-ang Toys and Spot-On models. It must have been a sad occasion for the firm that had been producing Meccano sets since 1907 and Dinky Toys for over thirty years. It was a surprising outcome, too, since the companies had been competitors at least since the 1930s, when Meccano had been the more successful of the two. Fortunately it enabled the production of Dinky Toys to continue for another fifteen years at Binns Road, although railway collectors suffered the loss of Hornby Trains, renamed Tri-ang-Hornby, with no further products manufactured in Liverpool. Lines Bros' own diecast-toy company, Spot-On, gradually disappeared over the next few years, with the Dinky Toys name being preferred.

The takeover did not affect production very greatly, although there were months when no new models were announced. 1963 had been the year with the highest number of new releases, almost thirty, although many of these were sets or re-releases in a different livery. Either this one final effort to build sales or the increasing cost of manufacture was their financial downfall. Virtually all the cars now possessed the new features that had been introduced since 1958. They were extremely sophisticated, and the Dinky Toys advertisement in the July 1967 edition of the *Meccano Magazine* (this was the final publication in its original format) illustrated ten modern cars, all with opening doors, boots and bonnets, and including two with wire wheels. They were no longer toys but true model cars, built to a high standard and boxed in strong, transparent plastic cases.

In this same advertisement the first two Thunderbirds toys, Lady Penelope's FAB 1 and Thunderbirds 2 & 4, were announced, heralding another new departure for Dinky Toys – television-related toys. These continued to the end of production and possibly delayed the final closure of the factory for a few months.

A unique departure for Dinky occurred in 1966 when a series of

Television- and film-related toys (from top left): Lady Penelope's FAB 1 (100); Thunderbirds 2 (101); Thunderbirds 2 & 4 (101); 'The Prisoner' Mini-Moke (106); Stripey the Magic Mini (107); Tiny's Mini-Moke (350); the Pink Panther (354); Parsley's Car (477); Dinky Beats (486). From 'Thunderbirds', 'Enchanted House' and other television series and films of the late 1960s and early 1970s.

American cars was manufactured under licence in Hong Kong. An article in *Meccano Magazine* vigorously defended the action of producing Dinky Toys abroad, but neither this foray nor later experiments were successful.

It is sad to chart the decline of any company, and particularly that of Meccano (1971) Ltd (the new name of the company), which was striving to discover a successful product that would save it from extinction. Throughout the 1970s several new ventures were tested, mostly without long-term success.

● 1969 (June). Speedwheels (plastic wheels with thin axles for extra speed): a belated attempt to compete with Mattel's Hotwheels, which had been introduced in 1967. Mattel were eventually to inherit the Dinky Toy trademark in 1996.

● 1971. The production in Britain of French-designed models, e.g. Citroën Dyane, Matra 630, Fiat Abarth 2000, Ferrari 312P, which had recently been manufactured in France. The first of thirty-one Metal Kits.

● 1972. The start of the production of very basic models again (back to toys), with simple castings and no features, such as the Bedford Royal Mail Van (410), which also ran on the ugly new unrealistic Speedwheels.

● 1972. The Van (410) casting was also supplied in various factory-sprayed colours without advertising to dealers, who then applied their own transfers. This was another innovation for Dinky Toys and illustrated how desperate they were for business.

Bedford CF Vans of the 1970s, including rare versions, Belaco (rear), Marley (rear) and Simpsons (left), with factory-sprayed models in black, white and red (centre front) supplied to intermediaries for the application of individual transfers.

Later buses including AEC Routemaster (four versions); Leyland Atlantean (three versions); AEC Merlin (two); and Standard Atlas (two). The Routemasters in boxes were produced as the factory was closing, including rare gold and silver versions.

Such a step would never have been permitted in the buoyant 1950s.

● 1972. Consolidation of two earlier developments in the military field. Half of the 1972 new issues consisted of the larger aeroplanes series (commenced in 1965) and the larger- scale military vehicles (commenced in 1968). Meccano obviously thought that war-orientated toys would appeal to boys. Compared to the previously mentioned Bedford Van, these combat models were brimming with details and features; however, they did cost considerably more. Perhaps the company was aiming at both markets to gauge which was the most profitable.

● 1973. Much of this year's production was reissues of previous models in different liveries. A low point in Dinky Toy history was the first issue of a new series of larger-scaled boats, which ran on wheels and could not float. Since these half-dozen boats were manufactured only for two or three years their abundant availability in toy shops well into the 1980s indicated their unpopularity, especially among collectors. Another experimental range: three 1:25 scale Ford Capris.

● 1974. This year produced the lowest number of new issues for twenty-three years, and again with a number of reissues. The writing was on the wall.

● 1975. Another poor year, with the majority of new models in 1974 and 1975 depicting military vehicles.

● 1976. In attempting to cash in on film-related toys the company produced Cinderella's coach in conjunction with a newly released film, *The Slipper and the Rose*. Neither was a success, and, like the boats, the coach had very limited appeal and was still available in shops for many years afterwards.

● 1977. One last attempt at something different brought the company to its lowest point with the introduction of very basic cheap children's toys – the Convoy Truck range. These were unidentified, identical chassis/cabs combined with alternative plastic bodies. About seven different versions were available, all running on Speedwheels. They were still in production when the factory closed, and another six were advertised to be released from 1980, but none of these was issued. Silver Jubilee buses and a taxi were also produced.

● 1978. Desperation this year brought five sets, four more Convoy Trucks and several reissues.

● 1979. This was the final year of production at the Binns Road factory. Products included two cardboard building kits, a Rover made in Hong Kong, a Volvo made in Italy, the inevitable reissues and sets, and a model of a Spitfire aircraft, which is now highly sought after, mainly because of its extremely short production run. It was a specially boxed

Final offerings. Most of these toys were in production at the time of the factory closure, including 180 Rover 3500 (made in Hong Kong) and 243 Volvo Police Car (made in Italy).

Diamond Jubilee RAF Spitfire in chrome and mounted on a plinth. It even had a special number, 700, the first in the Dinky Toy aeroplane series. On 30th November 1979 the Binns Road factory closed.

● 1980. Just a few re-liveried models and some odd imports, together with previously held stock, filtered into many unlikely retailing outlets during the early 1980s. This was the ignominious end of a fine diecasting toy company. It could not compete with cheap toy imports and the growing interest in computers and other more sophisticated toys.

In 1988, after the Dinky Toys brand name had been purchased by Universal International of Hong Kong, this company commenced the manufacture in China and Macau of thirty-two models in 1:43 scale called The Dinky Collection. They were attractive models of cars, vans and one coach (1:50 scale).

Between 1931 and 1980 more than one thousand different models had been produced in the United Kingdom. This total excludes all the overseas products, of which there was a similar number, as well as the many variations. So either starting or consolidating a collection of Dinky Toys is a huge challenge in terms not only of numbers of models and their storage but also of their current values. Nevertheless, collecting Dinky Toys is one of the fastest-growing hobbies, and the rarest items, now over seventy years old, like valuable antiques, are not only highly sought after but sell for high prices when they appear at auctions. Dinky Toys, the invention of Frank Hornby and the product of a modest factory in Binns Road, Liverpool, will go down in history as some of the most successful and collectable toys ever made.

Models from the 1950s, including twelve military vehicles, eight American two-tone sedans with later paint applications (destined mainly for the United States), and seven farm vehicles in rare colours.

39

FURTHER READING

Ellenbroek, Jan. *The Dinky Toy Collection.* Privately published, 2002.
Fawdry, Marguerite. *British Tin Toys.* New Cavendish Books, 1990.
Force, Ed. *Dinky Toys.* Schiffer, 2002.
Foster, Michael. *Hornby Dublo Trains.* New Cavendish Books, 1980.
Gardiner, Gordon. *Price Guide to Metal Toys.* Antique Collectors' Club, 1980.
Gardiner, Gordon. *Transport Toys.* Salamander, 1997.
Gardiner, Gordon, and Morris, Alistair. *Metal Toys.* Salamander Books, 1984.
Gibson, Cecil. *A History of British Dinky Toys.* Map Ltd, 1966; reprinted Mikansue, 1973.
Gibson, Cecil. *Commercial Vehicles (Models).* Thomas Nelson, 1970.
Greilsamer, Jacques. *Catalogue of Model Cars of the World.* Edita Lausanne, 1967.
Marshall, John. *Collecting Dinky Toy Aircraft.* Silverdale Press, 1973.
Ramsay, John. *British Diecast Model Toys Catalogue.* Swapmeet Publications, 2001.
Randall, Peter. *The Products of Binns Road – A General Survey.* New Cavendish Books, 1977.
Richardson, Mike and Sue. *Dinky Toys and Modelled Miniatures.* New Cavendish Books, 1981.
Richardson, Mike and Sue. *Giant Book of Dinky Toys.* New Cavendish Books, 2000.
Roulet, Jean-Michel. *Histoire des Dinky Toys Français.* Editions Adepte, 1978.
Stanford, Tony. *Meccano Magazine Digest.* Cranbourn Press, 1974.
Trench, Patrick. *Model Cars and Road Vehicles.* Pelham Books, 1983.
Williams, Guy. *The World of Model Cars.* André Deutsch, 1976.

PERIODICALS
Collectors' Gazette, Model Collector and *Diecast Collector,* all published monthly, always feature articles of interest and details of toy fairs and auctions. *Model Buses* is published every two months.

PLACES TO VISIT

Intending visitors are advised to check the opening times before travelling and to find out whether items of particular interest will be on display.

Bethnal Green Museum of Childhood, Cambridge Heath Road, London E2 9PA. Telephone: 020 8983 5200. Website: www.museumofchildhood.org.uk
Bressingham Steam Experience, Thetford Road, Bressingham, Diss, Norfolk IP22 2AB. Telephone: 01379 687386. Website: www.bressingham.co.uk (Houses the David Cooke Collection.)
Cotswold Motoring Museum and Toy Collection, The Old Mill, Bourton-on-the-Water, Gloucestershire GL54 2BY. Telephone: 01451 821255.
Coventry Toy Museum, Whitefriars Gate, Much Park Street, Coventry CV1 2LT. Telephone: 024 7622 7560.
Lakeland Motor Museum, Holker Hall and Gardens, Cark-in-Cartmel, Grange-over-Sands, South Lakeland, Cumbria LA11 7PL. Telephone: 01539 558509.
Museum of British Road Transport, Hales Street, Coventry CV1 1PN. Telephone: 024 7683 2425. Website: www.mbrt.co.uk (The Tiatsa Collection of toys and models.)
Museum of Childhood Memories, 1 Castle Street, Beaumaris, Anglesey LL58 8AP. Telephone: 01248 712498. Website: www.nwi.co.uk/museumofchildhood
National Motor Museum, John Montagu Building, Beaulieu, Brockenhurst, Hampshire SO42 7ZN. Telephone: 01590 612345. Website: www.beaulieu.co.uk (Limited number of items on display.)
Romney, Hythe and Dymchurch Toy and Model Museum, New Romney Station, New Romney, Kent TN28 8PL. Telephone: 01797 362353.

COLLECTORS' CLUBS AND OTHER ORGANISATIONS

Club Dinky France (CDF) (contact: Guy Girod), BP 5117, 14079 Caen Cedex 5, France.
Coventry Diecast Model Club (contact: John Print), Time Machine, 242 Abbey Road, Whitley, Coventry CV3 4BE. Telephone: 024 7645 7968.
D and J Fairs (contacts: John and Julie Webb). Telephone: 01526 398198. (Promoters of major toy and train fairs.)
Dinky Toys Collectors' Association, PO Box 60, Norwich NR4 7JF. (Enclose SAE) Email: davidcooke@tiscali.co.uk
London Toy and Model Collectors Club (contact: Lee Reynolds). Telephone: 01636 612542.
Maidenhead Static Model Club (contact: Michael Forbes). Telephone: 01933 665569.